How To Coach

FIELDING

How To Coach

FIELDING

Dr. A.K. Srivastava

M.P.Ed., N.I.S. (Athletics), D.Y. Ed., Ph.D. (Phy. Edu.)
Director, Physical Education
Delhi Engineering College, Bawana Road, Delhi-110042

OXSTALLS LEARNING CENTRE
UNIVERSITY OF GLOUCESTERSHIRE
Oxstalls Lane
Gloucester GL2 9HW
Tel: 01242 715100

SPORTS PUBLICATION

7/26, Ground Floor, Ansari Road, Darya Ganj,
New Delhi-110 002. Ph.: (O) 55749511, 55257538
(M) 9868028838 (R) 27562163

Published by:

SPORTS PUBLICATION
H.O.: 7/26, Ground Floor, Ansari Road,
        Darya Ganj, New Delhi-110 002.
Ph. : (O) 55749511, 55257538 (R) 27562163, (M) 9868028838
E-mail: *ektathani@hotmail.com/ lakshaythani@hotmail.com*
Website : www.sportspublication.trade-india.com

© 2006 Publishers

I.S.B.N. – 81-7879-233-8

PRINTED IN INDIA 2006

Laser Typeset by:
JAIN MEDIA GRAPHICS, Delhi-110035. Ph.: 27190244

Printed by:
CHAWLA OFFSET PRINTERS, Delhi-110052

Price: Rs. 140/-

PREFACE

How to Coach Fielding is specially written for the young aspiring cricketers and sportsperson who wish to learn, develop and sharp their fielding skills which is an integral aspects of cricket sport. Throughout the book, the fielding skills, tactics, techniques, fielding rules accompanied by latest court dimensions and measurements are explained in a lucid form and in simple colloquial English along with relevant illustrations for better understand the fielding skills and techniques.

By going through this book, any aspirant learner may definitely understand and sharp his fielding skills which is integral part of the game of cricket. It includes all the essentials ingredients of Fielding viz., skills, techniques, latest rules and court measurements and dimensions along with relevant illustrations.

The texts are critically arranged in such a manner that a learner feels ease while reading the texts and learning the skills, tactics, strategies, rules etc. of Fielding. The language used while composing the texts are basically simple colloquial English. The present study has a wide scope for everyone who wish to gain their knowledge towards this great game. Historical background, Skills, tactics, and techniques, latest amended rules with latest court dimensions and measurements are explained in lucid form and in a simple English keeping in mind the language difficulty of the students of physical education and sports science.

Hopefully, the present study will prove very handy and useful for the those involved in the field of physical education and sports specially cricket, prospective coaches, aspirant cricketer wish to develop his fielding skills, sports personalities, teachers, students of physical education, children as well as for the general readers. Thus, the present study has A-Z of Fielding which a cricketer, learner, aspirant player is looking for.

— **Dr. A.K. Srivastava**

CONTENTS

1

INTRODUCTION

In order to excel in the sport of cricket, the cricketer has to be thorough in the fielding technique. Once a learn perfected in the basic skills of fielding, he should perform practice regularly his fielding skills with regular exercises in order to be perfect and to get success in the fielding skills.

Fielding in Cricket is a ancient sports which is originally discovered in England and later developed and spread all over the world including Europe, Australia, USA and particularly in Asia. It is the most famous sport which has rapidly spread all over the world and gained its popularity at peak after soccer being the first famous world sport.

Fielding is just as important and can be just as attractive as batting or bowling. Many matches are won or lost as much by the standard of fielding, as by the actual strength of the batting or the bowling. What is more delightful to watch is a fielding side which by initiative, concentration and anticipation, dismisses batsmen by brilliant catching, and which displays consistently safe and clean handling to prevent run, and speedy and accurate returns to the wicket to effect run outs.

A fielder should go to the position desired by his Captain or bowler and stay there. He should not stray about. Remember, the bowler is bowling to the field he has set, not to the one to which the fielders have wandered.

After going to his allotted place in the field, he should show an intelligent interest in the game and expect every ball bowled to be hit to him. He should try to anticipate the batsman's stroke and keep an eye on his Captain. He may wish to move him without the batsman knowing.

Fielder should be ready to move to his next position at the end of an over. If the fielder is instructed to field on the boundary, then he should go to the boundary and not stand ten yards inside it. It is easier to run forward to take a catch than to run backwards, and it is also easier to narrow the angle to cut off a boundary hit from the boundary line than from a position ten yards inside it. The first and second slip fielders should watch the ball from the bowlers hand on to the bat, and the third slip and gully, being wider, should watch the bat.

All the fielders near the wicket should once they are down in a half crouching positions, stay there until they either have to field the ball or until it has reached the wicket-keeper or been played away. Those fielders away from the wicket, on the other hand, will start to move in as the bowler approaches the wicket. The ball should always be returned to the wicket-keeper, unless the fielder is close to the bowler.

Once the ball is in wicket-keeper's hand, it is dead. If a ball is thrown at the wicket-keeper, the fielder near and behind the wicket-keeper should always back up, in case the keeper misses the ball or the thrower makes a wide throw. There is nothing so annoying as a bad throwing that lands outside the wicket-keeper's reach and, because no fielder has backed up, causes extra runs.

When a ball is thrown at the bowler's end, it is the duty of the fielders near that wicket to rush up and gather the ball to make a run out. A bowler should be saved from taking fast throws as there is a possibility of his getting hurt which would make him unfit to bowl effectively or take further part in the game. Be careful with the new ball. Always return it full toss. Do not let it hit the ground.

A good fielder will enjoy his cricket and can get a great deal of satisfaction when he comes off the field if he knows he has saved runs for his side or made a catch which may prove a match winner.

Cricket is being played on a circular or an oval-shaped field. The area situated at the centre of the field is called *the pitch*. At the both end of the cricket pitch, two sets of wickets are situated. Three sets of vertical sticks together are called *the wicket*. Normally, a wicket is about 6-7 inches in breadth and about 3 feet in length.

The cricket pitch is designed and constructed in such a manner that it can afford the bounce generated by the cricket ball. The equator of the ball consisted of the seam of the ball. The bat which is an important instrument of a batsman is a paddle shaped instrument which is used by the batsmen in order to hit the ball thrown by the bowlers. Normally, batsmen used to choose their bats of their own style which is convenient and easier for them to play with.

There are three important ingredients of cricket viz., Batting, Bowling and Fielding. All have equal importance of their own. By the mixture of these three aspects, the sport of cricket is played. The players having good efficiency in batting skills are usually called the **batsmen**. While the players having excellent skills in the bowling are usually called the **bowlers**. On the other hand, there are players in the cricket sport who used to perfect in fielding skills are called as **fielders**. There are at least one specialist fielders who is called a wicketkeeper, four specialist bowlers and 5-6 specialist batsmen in a team side.

In the sport of cricket, the only one area in which all the cricketers should be efficient is the Fielding. Usually all the players either batsmen or bowlers have to equally field in the cricket. A batsman used to field when he is not batting, similarly, a bowler too has to field when he is not bowling.

Basically, there are two types of fielding which are planned by the two teams in cricket viz., close-in fielding and in the deep fielding. The close-in fielding is very similar to those in baseball called playing the infield. While the *in the deep fielding* resemble to the playing the outfield.

Usually, the close-in fielders used to stand at the distance of 10 feet from the batsman crease. No fielders other than wicketkeeper used to wear hand gloves and safety helmets.

The only objective of the fielders is to stop the ball hit by the batsman or from any sources i.e., leg byes, byes, over throw etc. The other objective of the fielders other than stopping the ball is to get the batsman out. The batsman will be called out by the field umpire if he plays loose stroke in the air and a fielder catches the ball, if the batsman is running between the wickets in order to get run and he is unsafe at the popping crease with the bat in the air he is declared out by the umpire. Thus, the fielders play their important role in order to cease the batsman from playing a long innings.

2

FIELDING ESSENTIALS

The fielding is one of the important aspects of the sport of cricket that a cricketer should know the skills, tactics and techniques of fielding.

The entire sequence of the event is described as follows:

The bowler used to bowl a ball from the non-striker's end near the umpire station, the batsman plays the ball into the gap between the fielders in order to score run, the fielder fields the ball and get back to the wicketkeeper who endeavous to breaks the wickets in order to get the batsman out before the batsman is unsafe at the crease. This is the only set of common sequence of events in the sport of cricket. But the pattern of the game may varies from ball to ball depending on the strokes played by the batsman and the bowling bowled by the bowlers.

The fielders have to keep in their mind the various strategies and fielding drills while fielding at the ground. The fielders should always look at the batsman stroke and are able to study the body language of the batsman i.e., where he will play his stroke and in which area of the field.

The following are some important tactics, techniques and strategies of the fielding which a fielders should always follow :

1. The fielders should be very alert and keep moving their body positioning while fielding on the cricket ground.

2. They should always keep their eyes on the ball.

3. They should make themselves sure that their body is behind the ball so that they are able to stop the ball from crossing the fence and to stop the extra runs scored by the batsman's stroke.

4. The fielders should always field with both hands instead of by one hand only in order to avoid some severe injuries.

5. The fielders should be very careful while throwing the ball to the appropriate destination and always throw the ball to the right end of the pitch.

6. The fielders should always throw the ball with accurate efficiency to the right end and never throw the ball with lose grip to score some extra runs from overthrow.

7. There is a tendency among the players to adhere their own style of fielding.

8. The fielders should chase the ball by following the specific technique, he should run towards the ball by turning slightly so that one shoulder is towards the ball. The fielder should go down on one knee, the knee that is toward the ball so that your leg is perpendicular to the motion of the ball. Then collect the ball carefully.

In this way, the fielder stops the ball played by the batsman. Often, when a batsman plays a shot, the ball spins. Due to this the ball may, on landing, change direction quite dramatically. The fielder has to account for this spin while fielding.

Anticipation is the key in fielding well. The fielder should walk towards the batsman while the bowler bowled the ball as it helps the fielders to be in motion because starting off from a complete stop takes more time and energy.

It is not possible for the fielders to attack at the ball rolling towards them with tremendous speed, in this case mostly fielders used to stop the ball with one hand or one leg; sometimes this stance will become useful tips for the fielders and they succeeded in cease the ball to cross the fence. In order to get thorough on fielding drills, the fielders needs regular practice.

One very useful matter to consider is that the playing field is often uneven and the ball might bounce unexpectedly. The fielders should always leave themselves some leeway while blocking the ball. Again, here the fielders should keep their eyes on the ball is critical. Throwing accurately over the wicket is another critical part of the game.

The wicketkeeper does not appreciate wild and wayward throws. A flat fast throw over the wicket is ideal. A great deal of practice is needed before a player has an accurate throw.

While catching and fielding, the fielders should follow the specialised techniques of catching and fielding the ball which are as follows:

1. The fielders should always use their two hands as much as possible while catching.

2. The fielders should take appropriate positioning while fielding specially while catching, he should

cup his hands with cup grip in order to make a soft catch instead of harder one.

3. The fielder should take necessary precautions in order to make a soft catch to avoid the ball from bouncing out of the fielder's hands.

4. The fielder should make the cup of hands by interlocking the thumbs and keeping the little finger towards the ball, if the ball is above chest height.

5. The fielder should always get under the ball as far as possible while catching.

6. When the ball is above chest height, the fielder should endeavour to stand such that the ball moves directly in the direction of his face.

7. If the ball seems to move beyond the fielder, he should not run backwards the ball.

8. If the ball coming towards the face of the fielder, he should turn around and make attempt by getting under the ball rather than over the ball.

9. It will be recommended for the fielders to run after the ball by his front foot and should run forward instead of backward.

All the above mentioned drills will proved very beneficial for the fielders in the deep.

The following are some specific techniques which are recommended for the close-in fielders:

1. The fielders fielding at the close-in zone should be relaxed and anticipated which usually plays an important role in close-in fielding.

2. The close-in fielders should overcome the fear of hurting by the ball, this situation will be well explained by the sports psychologist or the team

coach before the play of the a match.

3. The close-in fielders should always keep their eyes on the ball.

4. While fielding, the close-in fielders should take the ball on the fleshy part of their hand rather than on the bony part.

5. The close-in fielders should take appropriate precautions pertaining their fingers as there always a chance of injuries pertaining fingers.

3

BALL RETURNING

In an average day's first-class cricket, a certain number of overs are bowled. The number will naturally vary according to the type of bowler who is operating but there may be 400 or even 600 deliveries. If we eliminate the first ball when it is often hand to him, and the last ball, it still leaves possibly some 400 times a day that the ball is returned to the bowler.

From these perhaps 25 per cent come back from the wicket-keeper, but it is reasonable to assume that various fieldsmen have to return the ball to the bowler 200 to

300 times a day. It becomes clear that this movement can have a bearing on how tired the bowler becomes by stumps. Once a bowler who had just completed over 50 overs in the one innings, and was almost ready to drop, being forced to hastily stoop and pick up a nasty return which came from all fieldsman less than ten yards away. It was not because of any lack of thought or sympathy but merely because of a bad method of returning the ball.

In their anxiety to drop the ball softly right in the bowler's lap, so many chaps throw it back lolly-pop fashion. If there is an error of judgement and the ball falls short, it causes the, bowler to stoop and pick up an awkward return. Any risk of this can be avoided by adopting a different method or a different trajectory. These remarks are intended to apply only to return from fieldsmen who are short distances from the bowler.

Standing Positions

It is always difficult to be absolutely sure of the correct fielding position but we may safely adhere to sensible deductions. In the outfield it is recommended that the man who is placed on the fence should stand at least five yards inside. It is obvious that from such a position no catch could go over the fielder's head and still land inside the boundary because he must have some time in which to observe its flight and move.

On the other hand he can certainly take a catch some five yards closer to the batsman than he could if standing right on the boundary line. The depth of mid-on or cover is largely determined by the tenor of play, pace of the ground, etc. Cover normally would stand as far back as possible consistent with being able to save a single. The depth of slip fields is often a problem. Player placed at cover had a good sight of the ball and could judge its carry. Quite often the fielders positioning at the slips are asked by the team captain to come up closer and many times was confronted with their view that they were getting too close to focus catches. Well, that's a fine point of judgement, but it is always better to miss a catch than not to have the opportunity of catching it all because the ball fell short. Another important thing about slips of the width they stand apart. First slip should be well clear-of the wicket-keeper.

The keeper should take what catches he can, and when he is standing back to a fast bowler he can cover a lot of ground. If a keeper is able to take catches which would have gone to first slip, then first slip is too fine. He should stand just so wide that in his judgement a catch won't go between him and the keeper. Then, of course, the other slips adjust their position with him. In all cases they should stand as far apart as possible whilst making sure catches won't go between. Second slip a little closer to the bat then first slip and third slip a little closer than second slip. It is natural that the finger a siip catch the less resistance off the bat and the further carry.

The gully fieldsman will have to adjust his place according to whether he is aiming to take a catch off a defensive prod, such as might happen on a sticky, or a full blooded cut on a firm pitch. To take the latter very close in is no fun. Cover is the place for a specialist, who should be able to move fast and throw well.

The underhand throw is valuable for him because he frequently has to get rid of the ball whilst on the run and no fieldsman is so likely to receive opportunities for run-outs. Fieldsmen at cover, point, gully or third-man should remember that practically every stroke which is hit to them by a right-hand batsman will be partially cut and therefore will tend to curve from their right side towards their left. They should endeavour, where possible, to field the ball on their right-hand side, so that any curl to the left can be controlled. But if the ball is being taken on the left side and goes away, you are in real trouble. Many inexperienced fieldsman at point has caused a laugh by failing to make allowance for this spin.

To a much lesser degree on-side fieldsmen will find the ball tending to go from their left-hand side towards their right. Only in the case of an off-spinner who is really breaking it will this curve be pronounced on the leg side and it is likely to be more so for shots hit behind square-leg. All fielding and catching should be performed with both hands whenever possible. Some fellows like to be flash and show how smart they are with one hand. It doesn't pay.

The fielders should take appropriate precautions while fielding with one hand when there is no other option left depending on the type of situation. Care should be taken from the very first ball of the match to guard against mistakes. When a game is lost by one tun or one wicket it is usually the last mistake which is remembered and that poor fieldsman hounded. Memories are sometimes short. It may have been a quite unnecessary piece of foolishness two days before that really caused the damage. Close-in fielders must naturally keep still whilst the bowler is running up to bowl and on delivery. This is most important for men at say short-leg and silly point where any movement would district the batsman. But mid-off, cover and the outfields should always start to move in as the bowler commences his run. It makes a tremendous difference to be on the move.

When fielding a ball defensively, it is wise to use your body or legs as a protective shield. Get in front of the ball so that an unexpected bounce or turn won't get past. But when it comes to the chance of a run-out this method may be too slow and something different is called for.

Very often there is no chance of positioning oneself at all. It is a case of do the best you can. But sometimes in from the outfield is a case it is possible to adjust one's run and get into the finest possible position for an accurate throw in one continuous action without losing a fraction of a second.

No fieldsman has any control over the speed of the batsman's shot and therefore, by judgement, your own speed and direction must so regulated that you reach the ball some six inches in front of and slightly to the right of the right toe. From this position the ball is gathered in both hands as the full weight of the body goes on to the right foot and it is transferred to the left as the throw takes place. If these directions are closely followed you can move so that not a moment is lost in gathering the ball and disposing of it.

The method can be used whether the fielder returns the ball with an underarm type of throw, round-arm or overarm. A fieldsman can usually judge whether the run-out will be touch and go or whether the batsman is at his mercy. Should it be the latter, always co-operate with wicket-keeper or fieldsman. Only when time is vital should you put everything into an effort to hit the stumps. Many a run-out has been a cinch but the fieldsman, by a wild throw at the 'keeper's shoe laces, has given him an impossible ball to take and the chance has been missed. Slip-fielding machines can be procured and these offer useful practice.

However, their value is rather limited because it becomes a relatively easy matter to tell which way the ball will go after hitting the wooden slats. The fielder can thus anticipate its direction, something he can very seldom do with safety on the field of play. Every fieldsman should remain alert and be as active as possible.

There should be no standing with arms folded or hands in pockets. No leaning against the fence. Talking to spectators or signing autographs over the fence are not the thing to do in big cricket. They may be harmless but they are distracting and tend to upset concentration. Where there is a slip-fielding specialist in a team, he should be used in the slips. There is no position in the field where catches are so numerous or so difficult.

4

IMPORTANT FIELDING TIPS

The following are some fielding coaching tips which a fielder has to follow in order to be a perfect fielder :

1. Defensive Fielding

The one of the important goal of the fielder is to stop the ball and cease the batsman to score run. This is called the defending fielding. Due to the time required to get the ball for throwing, the old technique of defending the ball by slightly bent the knees is gradually become unpopular and it is only left for the bad outfielders.

For the quick sequence of fielding, the modern defensive fielding technique is used to follow by the fielders in which there is no need of bent down the knees for holding the ball but just bent little bit for holding the ball. The fielder should watch the ball closely at all the times until the ball may come into the fielder's hand without making any haste to avoid grabbling.

2. Throwing

After stopping the ball the second motive of the fielder to throw the ball into the appropriate end of the pitch to the bowler or to the wicketkeeper.

For throwing the ball the fielder should have the appropriate body balance with an accurate throw.

The fielder should throw the ball over the shoulder with a vertical arm if the distance is long and go for the sideways throw when distance is short and time crucial.

In cases of runout. Very important to keep that wrist firm behind the ball. You will be surprised how much load it takes of your shoulder.

Throw over the shoulder with a vertical arm if the distance is long and go for the sideways throw when distance is short

The misconception going around is the lesser you throw, longer the arm stays good. Kapil Dev has proved this theory to be completely false. Kapil threw frequently, even in net sessions, forget matches. He believed, by keeping that arm active you make it stronger plus, you also do not surprise your arm by suddenly throwing in a match. This in fact assures you of an injured throwing arm. Correct that throwing technique and keep throwing frequently. Thats the idea.

The ball should be watched right into the hands before the arms begin to move for the throw. It is not advisable to look up too soon. The right foot is at right angles to the intended line of the throw and the knee is slightly bent. Stretch the right hand backwards with the elbow bent. The left hand, the left shoulder and the left foot point towards the target. With a swift swing of the right hand release the ball.

As the ball is being released, the weight of the body is transferred to the left foot and the right shoulder points towards the target. While it is not a good thing, especially for a beginner to specialize too seriously on one or two positions in the field, each member of a cricket team is likely to possess certain physical attributes which automatically fit him for some positions better than others. Captain has to decide which player has to position where on the field keeping in mind his general qualities.

3. The Cup (Hands)

The most commonly fielding techniques to catch the ball is the two cup of hands. Usually one cup is where the 2 little fingers are overlapping to ensure that there is

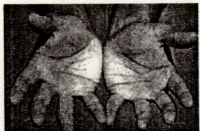

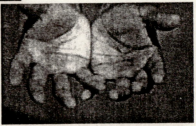

no overlapping of fingers while attempting to catch. The two cup of hands are usually adhere by the fielders positioning at the slips. In order to avoid any give or break through whenever the ball hits the area, the fielder should not overlap the other fingers at the other cup.

In the two cups of hands with no overlapping, the fielder has option to use the either method but the only motive of the fielder is to make a big cup for taking appropriate catch.

The fielder should let the ball hit the base of the fingers on the palm, which means on reflex the fingers close on the ball. The fielder should look to receive the ball with soft palms. Instead of snatching the ball, the fielder should let the ball melt into his hands by correct positioning the body.

In order to be perfect catcher, the fielder should perform relevant practice at least 100 catches a day as recommended by the legend fielders like Jhonty Rhodes and Mohammed Azharuddin etc.

4. Close Catching

The fielders fielding at the close-in fielding zone should take their relevant positions by keeping eyes on the ball hit by the batsman's bat. The catchers should avoid becoming set as the muscles may stiffen and slow down by their reaction time.

The fielder should not stand too close to the batsman in order to avoid any grabbling and injuries. The fielder should avoid a really wide stance or too narrow a stance. The following are some coaching tips for the fielders in order to make the close catch :

1. The fielders should not stay on the heels while catching but should be well balanced and alert to react into any direction.

2. The fielder should stay lower particularly on the low bounce pitches and vice versa.

3. The fielder should not get up in the knees before the ball come to him this may provide him a lot of help to him.

4. The fielder should react only when he is fully ensure pertaining the position of the ball coming towards him.

5. The fielder should react at the appropriate time while close catching.

6. The fielder should be very alert while standing at the slip area for taking close catch and should always keep his eyes on the batsman's bat and should watch the outer edge of the bat while standing at the slips.

7. The fielder should always concentrate harder in the close-in position.

The above said coaching tips will help the close-in fielder to be thorough and perfect in the fielding skills.

5. High Catches

One of the most exciting sights at a cricket ground is that when the batsman flick the ball up high into the sky and a fielder is getting under it.

More catches are dropped by not getting into correct position than by the failure of hands to grip the ball. The basic technique to hold a high catch is:

a. Get perfectly balanced and keep the head still with eyes intensely watching the ball;

b. When the ball is about to touch the hands which have been formed into a cup, get them down towards the chest, at the same time folding the fingers over the ball. If the hands are kept still at the time of ball touching the hands, the ball will jump out of the hands.

c. Try to catch the ball at eye level;

d. Get under the line of the ball as soon as possible;

e. Keep the eyes glued to the ball until it is safe into the hands;

f. Open the hands and fingers and keep the hands as near as possible to catch other. Do not keep the fingers and palms stiff but relax them;

Can be quite unnerving for a fielder though for it is quite a while that he stays under the ball, ample time for all kinds of thoughts to run through the mind. The temperament of a cricketer is convincingly tested when he is taking a skier. A coach often puts a new student through this test. While taking high catch, the fielder go under it should always keep his eye on the ball and should bring his leg forward by keeping the body balance.

The fielder should not perform the high catch by stay on the heels. It also helps to react quickly if there is fumble. The cup of the hand should be at around the chest height and considered the ideal position. The fielder should run on the toes in case he is chasing and running for attempting a running skier catch.

The fielder should keep his head steady and should perform gliding running instead of sprinting with appropriate bodily balance which help the fielder while attempting the high catch. Lastly, the fielder should keep steady his head while attempting high catch rather than shake the head.

All the above mentioned tips will help the fielders successful in taking high catches.

6. Underarm Flick

In today's modern cricket, the underarm throw is called the underarm flick. The techniques of underarm throw has been changed over the past few decades. This particular area has gained so much momentum now-a-days with the advent of one day cricket.

In one day cricket, the fielders used to remain inside the 30 yards circle flicking underarm to get a crucial run out and changing the complexion of the game. The fielder in order to save time should collect the ball in front of him rather than besides him and with a flick of the wrist instead of the unwinding of the arm, as the older method. The fielder should not look up at the target unless until the ball is into his hand as this may create the fumble.

5

FIELDING
POSITIONS

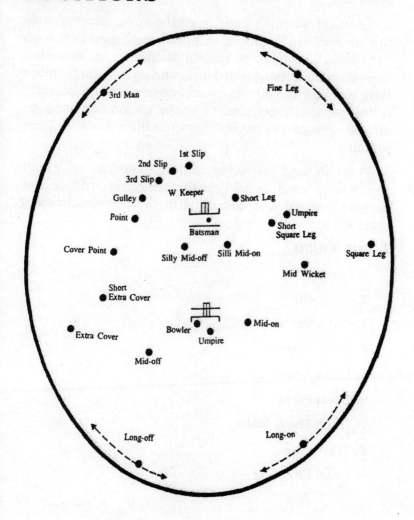

Cricket is team sport which consisted of 12 players in both teams. Out of 12 players, only 11 players used to play with one player kept reserved for substitution.

Out of the 11 players on the field, one player act as a wicketkeeper, one player resume the position of a bowler, the remaining players keep the position of the different positions on the field as imparted by the team captain according to the bowler.

The field placings used to change over usually after the interval and beginning of a new over depending upon the bowler's tactics and the situation around. The team captain is the ultimate authority and each team member have to follow the directions and orders of the captain; it is the captain's decision to either go for defensive or attacking outfields depending upon the situation of the match.

The following are some fielding positions on which the fielders used to field on the cricket ground on the captain's signal and according to the bowler's bowling tactics :

I. OUT-FIELD

1. Long-Off
2. Long-On
3. Deep Mid-Off
4. Deep Extra
5. Extra Cover
6. Deep Point
7. Deep Third Main
8. Third Man
9. Deep Fine Leg

10. Long Leg

11. Deep Square Leg

12. Deep Mid Wicket

13. Deep Mid On

II. IN-FIELD

1. Mid-off

2. Mid-on

3. Mid Wicket

4. Short Extra Cover

5. Cover Point

6. Backward Point

7. Point

8. Gully

9. Short Third Man

10. Short Fine Leg

11. Backward Square Leg

12. Square Leg

III. CLOSE-IN-FIELD

1. First Slip

2. Second Slip

3. Third Slip

4. Fourth Slip

5. Silly Point

6. Silly Mid-off

7. Short Mid-off

8. Short Mid-on

9. Silly Mid-on

10. Forward Short Leg

11. Backward Short Leg

12. Leg Slip

I. OUT-FIELD

This is the outermost zone of the cricket field consisted of about thirteen (13) fielding positions which are as follows :

1. Long-Off

This is the important position located at the outfield. The area situated at the offside of the batsman's position near the boundary. Usually, players having good height used to field there because there are chances of batsman out by catch the ball.

2. Long-On

This is the important position located at the outfield. The area situated at the legside of the batsman's position near the boundary. Usually, players having good height used to field there because there are chances of batsman out by catch the ball. In one day cricket, this position becomes particularly important because during the last 10 overs, the batsmen used to score big runs by hitting boundaries and sixes and one loose stroke will cause their wicket by catch by the long-on fielder.

3. Deep Mid-Off

This position is situated at the outfield. The area situated at the offside of the batsman's position near infield zone is known as Deep Mid-Off. The player fielding at this area should be very alert as there are great chances of the batsman hit at that area. Mostly in one day cricket, during the last overs to go, the captain used to arrange his players into that area in order to stop runs and getting the batsman out.

4. Deep Extra

This position is situated at the outfield. The area situated at the offside of the batsman's position near infield zone besides the deep mid-off area is called the deep extra. This area is also important appropriate attention should be given by the fielders in order to be thorough in fielding drills while standing at this area.

5. Extra Cover

Another outfield area situated near the Deep Extra. The fielder fielding at this area should remain alert all the times the batsman played the stroke.

6. Deep Point

This area too the part of out-field in cricket. The zone between extra cover and deep third man is called as Deep Point. The fielder positioned at this area should be very keen to hold the ball coming towards him.

7. Deep Third Man

The area near third man and next to Deep Point is called as Deep Third Man. The fielder fielding at this area should have athletic flexibility in order to move to hold the ball passing by him to save the runs.

8. Third Man

This area also comes under out-field. Third Man is an important fielding position situated before Deep Third Man. Usually, captain employed only one fielder at Deep Third Man or Third Man in order to stop runs or catching position.

9. Deep Fine Leg

Deep Fine Leg is also out-field position. It is situated before short fine leg area. Very rarely captain employed his fielders at this area depending upon the circumstances of the match.

10. Long Leg

An outfield area just parallel to short fine leg. This area is very important because mostly batsmen used to sweep the spin bowlers at this area in order to get a boundary or sixes. The fielder fielding at this area should be very keen to hold the ball.

11. Deep Square Leg

It is another important outfield area which is situated before square leg. Generally leg umpire used to stand besides this area watching the situation from leg side. The batsman strong in leg side used to play stroke at this area in order to score runs in the form of boundaries and sixes, so the fielder fielding at this area should be very alert and always keep his eyes on the ball coming towards him.

12. Deep Mid Wicket

It is yet another outfield zone which is situated before mid-wicket. The fielder positioned at this area should be perfect in fielding skills viz., throwing, and specially taking catches as there are great chances of batsman play the loose stroke in the air in his effort to score boundaries and sixes.

13. Deep Mid-On

It is another outfield area which is situated between deep mid wicket and long-on zone. The fielder fielding at this particular area should have athletic flexibilities as the batsmen used to play their authentic strokes to this area in order to get runs.

II. IN-FIELD

This is another important fielding zone situated just next to out-field zone. There are about twelve (12) fielding positions in in-field zone. Each positions have their relevant place in fielding. Some of the in-field positions are cover point, mid-wicket, square leg etc., and those who are positioned in similar positions specially in the one day cricket matches who used to field at the edge of the 30 yard circle are the quickest and very often a team's best fielders. The in-field fielders should have the appropriate agilities viz., one-handed pick-up at speed, combined with early and accurate throwing abilities etc. The following are the brief discussions pertaining these twelve (12) fielding positions :

1. Mid-Off

This is an important position in every class of cricket, because it is such a good place for a captain to field. From mid-off, the captain can so easily advise and encourage the bowler. His exact position will vary slightly according to the batsman and the bowler; thus for a defensive batsman, mid-off can move up to within about 18 yards of the bat, but for a strong attacking batsman he is usually 25 to 30 yards away. His main job is to stop and hold all the off-drives within his reach.

Many balls which are well pitched up and in the vicinity of the off stump will be hit hard and firmly along the ground in mid-off's direction. If these are mistimed slightly, a possible catch will often result, but it is likely to be a hard catch, hard in the sense that the ball will be travelling fast rather than one requiring acrobatic ability to reach and hold it.

Many mid-offs are solidly built fellows with large tough hands. Yet they cannot afford to be solid and inactive because they must be ready to dash in a counter the semi-defensive push stroke which sends the ball slowly in their direction and gives the batsman a quick run if mid-off is a slow starter.

2. Mid-On

One of the few places on the cricket field where it is possible to hid a poor fielder is mid-on. Like his counter-part, mid-off, the exact position he occupies will vary according to circumstances, but unlike mid-off, he will have far fewer drives to stop or catches to hold. The reason is simply that it is easier for a batsman to drive a ball on the off-side, the bad balls outside the leg stump being generally placed more squarely in the direction of the umpire or mid-wicket.

3. Mid-Wicket

It is important in-field zone which is situated between silly mid-on and deep mid-wicket. A good fielder should be employed at this fielding position as there are great chances of batsman to play his relevant stroke at this area.

4. Short Extra

It is import in-field positions situated besides the cover point. Usually batsman hit the ball to this position in order to get single run, so the fielder should keep himself very alert all the times on the field and specially when the batsman is about to play the ball.

5. Cover Point

Probably more run-outs result from the cover point position than from any other part of the field. The distance the cover fieldsman in that position should be the quickest mover and the most accurate short distance thrower in the team. He must learn to anticipate each stroke by watching the direction of each delivery and the movements of the batsman's feet. If he plays forward to a ball well pitched up, he should not move in too quickly as a hard hit at cover may easily beat the fieldsman.

If he plays back, then he should move in quickly to prevent a possible short single, as the ball is less likely to be hit hard in back play. A ball driven to cover seldom maintains a straight line but usually spins away in a direction to the left of the fieldsman if driven by the right handed batsman.

The other specialist fielding positions are near the batsman, i.e., silly-mid-off, silly-mid-on, short square leg and short fine leg. These fielders have got to be alert all the time and above all they have got to be courageous, active and sure catchers. They should not try to move away the head when the batsman is about to swing his bat. They should keep an eye on the bat until the batsman has played the ball.

6. Backward Point

An in-field zone situated between the cover point and point. The fielder fielding at this position should be very alert as there are wide scope of runs scored by the batsman by hitting the ball towards this position. Usually, a fielder having perfect in fielding drills should be placed at this location.

7. Point

Another in-field position situated between the backward point and short third-man next to gully. The fielder fielding at this area should be well versed in fielding skills and should have abilities to pick-up and throw the ball at speed by one-hand to the appropriate destination.

8. Gully

It is an important in-field position in cricket. The fielder positioning at this position should have athletic flexibilities as there always the possibilities of ball coming to this end as the batsman in order to hit the off-stump ball to the fence to score runs.

9. Short Third-Man

Speed round the boundary edge, ability to pick up on the run and accurate long-distance, throwing are the main requisites for third man. Catches are comparatively rare in this position, but, as third man often goes to long field at the end of the over, it is a mistake to imagine that he need not be a good catcher, for it is obviously impossible for any player to field at third man at both ends.

As a general principle, his chief task is to save the two, a cut or sliced drive in his direction will usually be a certain run, and it will become two runs if he hesitates before returning the ball to the wicket-keeper. Mentally, it is an easy position, because there is no need for great concentration on every ball.

10. Short Fine Leg

It is yet another in-field position which is situated between the short third-man and backward square leg. Usually, very rare strokes are played by the batsman at this end and hence, the poor fielders may also positioned at this end.

11. Backward Square Leg

This fielding position is situated next to leg slip area. It is an important fielding position and fielder appointed there should be very alert and have fielding efficiency skills as there are great chances of batsman hitting at this end.

12. Square Leg

Square leg is yet position at in-field area which requires appropriate attentions and efficient fielding skills as the batsman who is strong in playing leg side strokes used to hit the ball at this end.

III. CLOSE-INFIELD

This is a most important fielding zone situated just next to in-field zone. There are about twelve (12) fielding positions in close-infield zone. Each positions have their relevant place in fielding. The fielders of close-infield usually are the team's best and specialist fielders having fielding skills including one-hand throw at speed, with accurate follow through. Some of the important fielding positions in close-infield are forward short leg, silly point, silly mid-on, silly mid-off etc. The general aspects and outlook of the close-infield remains the same in today's cricket with the growing numbers of protective covering and equipments and facilities for the fielders who are fielding at the suicidal positions at close-infield.

The following are the brief discussions pertaining these twelve (12) close-infield positions :

1. First Slip

According to the type of bowler and the condition of the pitch, there may be one, two, three or even, very occasionally, four slips. Comparative immobility of foot, extraordinary quickness of eye, arms, hands, and fingers and intense concentration are the main attributes of a first class slip fielders.

The slip fielders should take up their positions where they feel ball will come to them at a convenient height if it is snicked by the batsman. Their feet should be spaced comfortably apart for balance, but not so far apart to prevent them springing sideways immediately off either foot.

Knees should be slightly bent with the body bent over to suit the height of the fieldsman. Hands should be kept easily in front of the body with the fingers relaxed and pointing slightly downwards.

The whole body should be slightly relaxed and ready for quick movement in any direction.

First slip should stand sufficiently wide of the wicket-keeper so that his vision will not be obstructed when the keeper has to move across to take a ball on the off side. Other slip fielders should be so placed that a ball played between them may be reached by either without colliding with the other.

2. Second Slip

The second slip fielder should be stand sufficiently wide of the first slip fielder so that his vision will not be obstructed by the first slip fielder. The fielder should stand in a position which suit his eye level and where he may better judge the ball edged from the batsman's bat.

3. Third Slip

The third slip fielder should be positioned sufficiently wide from the second fielder so that there may be less chances of the obstruction and collision among the slip fielders. Again, the third slip fielder should stand at the position away from the second slip fielder and from where he may judge the ball coming towards him.

4. Fourth Slip

The fourth slip fielder should take his positioned away from the third slip fielder. There should be enough gap between the third and fourth slip fielders as there always the chances of collision between the slip fielders while holding the ball or taking catch.

All slip fielders should be on the alert for a rebound from the keeper or from the hands of adjacent fieldsmen, and should be prepared to back up the keeper and attend the wicket if the latter happens to rush away to recover a ball which has been played a short distance away from the wicket.

5. Silly Point

This is one of the important close-infield position which is also called as suicidal position as there always be a danger of batsman playing the strokes towards the fielder positioned at the silly point area. But nowadays in modern cricket, with the amendment and advancement in the protective equipments and facilities for the fielders, there are less chances of fielders get hurt. The team's specialist fielders used to take this position depending upon the circumstances of the match.

6. Silly Mid-off

It is another close-infield position situated next to silly point. This area is very crucial and important from fielder's point of view. The batsman used to play at this end in order to get singles and play for long drive towards the silly mid-off fielder so the person appointed at this end should keep himself alert and should always keep his eyes on the ball coming towards him.

7. Short Mid-off

It is also as important as other close-infield positions such as silly point, silly mid-off etc., because the batsmen used to hit the ball in order to get single at this end. Usually, team's specialist and best fielders should be appointed at this end.

8. Short Mid-on

This position is very much appropriate to the team's captain leading the fielding team as the captain may provide his necessary advises and suggestions to the bowler and discuss with him the necessary precautions and match strategies.

9. Silly Mid-on

This location is situated between forward short leg and short mid on. Again team's best fielders usually appointed at this end as there always be the chances of the ball coming towards this end by the batsman in order to score run. The fielder fielding at this end should be very alert and should have athletic activities and flexibilities in order to hold the ball and take some extraordinary catches which may change the match outlook.

10. Forward Short-Leg

This is another important close-infield area which is situated next to silly mid-on. This is the most suicidal position in the cricket field as the fielder has to stand nearby the batsman who may play some attacking strokes which may hurt the fielders positioned at the forward short-leg area. In today's cricket with the advancement of the protective equipments and facilities, there are now less chances of the fielders get hurted as the fielder used to field there by wearing a safety helmet on the head but still this is an crucial and suicidal position in the cricket field.

11. Backward Short-Leg

It is situated near and next to forward short-leg area. Usually team's best and specialist fielder used to field at this end as the ball soundly hit by the batsman with full momentum used to pass by the fielder standing there. So, the fielders should be positioned there with wearing safety covering to avoid injuries. This is another suicidal position in the cricket field.

12. Leg Slip

It is yet another close-infield position which is situated near and besides the backward short-leg behind the wicketkeeper. The fielder having less and poor fielding efficiency may be placed at this end as the ball barely pass through this end.

6

PLACING THE FIELD

One of the important task of the team's captain is to place the field at the cricket ground. The field placement will depend after taking into account a number of variables viz., whether the opposite team are capable of chasing the team's total with the bunch of attacking batsmen; whether or not the fielding team has already batted and if so, whether the total runs they scored during their batting innings are decisive enough for the team's captain to judge the fielding team is in a winning position and so on.

Usually, the fielding team's captain always endeavour to set an attacking field so as to force the batting side into making errors by adopting aggressive bowling tactics and placing fieldsmen in close position to the batsman. The fielding captain will go for a defensive field if he observes that his team's previous batting total may be easily eclipsed by the opponent. The fielders should be positioned in such a manner that they would be able to save the runs scored by the batsmen particularly boundaries.

The captain should have the qualities of a judge to understand the capabilities and efficiencies of his team's member in order to allot them the appropriate fielding positions which would affectively impact on the opposite side and make it difficult task for the opponent to score the big total and in this way laying the foundation of the team' victory.

In one day cricket, during the first fifteen (15) overs, the fielding captain usually keep his best fielders in close-infield positions such as Silly Point, Silly Mid-on, Forward Short-Leg, First Slip, Second Slip etc., by discussing with the bowler. The field placement will definitely depends on the bowler's bowling tactics and batsman's capability and conscience. The bowler should bowl according to the fields placement so that the batsman will face difficulty in taking the singles and scoring the boundaries .

7

PHYSICAL FITNESS FOR THE FIELDERS

As the fielding job is usually tedious and a fielder on the field of cricket ground has to keep on move in the form of running, chasing the ball, performing catches, throwing etc. In order to keep themself physically fit and sound, the appropriate physical fitness is required for the fielders who has to keep on running and walking for at least 6 hours in the cricket field. To keep the players fit and in sound health, there is a provision of physician in a cricket team like in our cricket team, there is a team physician who is responsible for maintaining physical fitness among the players.

In order to keep themself fit and in sound health for taking participate in a match, the fielders have to undergo some training programmes which are managed by the team's physician :

1. Aerobic Training

The fielder should at least perform two sessions of about 45-60 minutes of aerobic training in a week. Usually, aerobic training consisted of exercises which are usually performed by the fielders at a low intensity. The fielder should be able to hold a little conversation, however should be finished with a good level of sweat. Cycling, rowing and running etc., are some good forms of aerobic exercises which should be performed by the fielders in order to keep themself physically fit.

If a fielder has a poor fitness level, he should work on spending 15 minutes on each of these three exercises viz., cycling, rowing and running. The fielders should be aimed to build up to 45 minutes plus on one of the disciplines. The aim here is not only to get fit whilst working for 45 minutes plus, but to also keep their mind busy and focused whilst performing a simple exercise, it may become lonely out on the boundaries.

2. Hand Eye Exercises

The fielders should collectively gather together as a team and should work in the nets, by performing simple throwing and catching drills which will help the neuro-muscular system. These should be practiced at all training sessions, but most importantly, prior to stepping on to the playing field. Fielders should throw the ball to each other, especially the slips, bats man should not sit around waiting to go on, the next 2 or 3 bats man in, should be stretching, warming up, and being bowled at - Rest is Rust.

3. Foot Exercises

Usually, foot exercises are used to gain speed in footwork. Some famous foot exercises which are exercised by the fielders such as : lay out a rope ladder, or chalk out an area with approximately 15 inch squares. Combining ladders so that the fielder go both forward and sideway's, will provide a fielder rapid results.

By performing these exercises in both directions, the fielder will soon realize that he is better on one side than the other. The fielder should aim to work on his weaker side for greater improvements in his game.

4. Speed Work

The fielder should look at the plyometric circuit to developing explosive power, he should aim to do this circuit no more than once a week, and certainly not on days before a match, as this type of circuit takes a few days to recover from.

5. Shuttle Sprints

Usually, most sprints last for between 6 and 40 meters in a match, so the fielder should look at this distance for his training. The fielder should work his sprints in the following form, standing start, running start, lying start i.e., walk forward for 4 steps then turn either to the side or completely behind for a short sprint. Once a fielder can complete these drills in normal training kit, he should work all the drills wearing all his pads and carrying his bat.

6. Upper Body

The fielder should perform the following session once a week in his competitive season, and ideally twice a week during the closed season, aiming to keep good form throughout the exercises. He should avoid taking the weight too heavy as this will result in gaining muscle bulk, rather than strength and speed. An excellent exercise in the form of Single Arm Triceps Pullover; this will stabilize the weighted arm with the fielder's free hand, whilst lifting the weight up, the fielder should keep his elbow pointing upwards. The fielder should perform 3 sets of 12-15 reps with a lightweight, at a 2-0-2 rate. The triceps muscle plays an important part in throwing of the ball, and also extending the arm in batting.

The fielder should perform bench fly's on either

inclined or flat bench, using dumbbells. He should remember not to allow his elbows to go lower than his shoulders, and should bring his hands together at the top, 3-0-2 rate 3 sets of 12 –15 reps same weight. If the fielder's bench can decline and incline, he should aim to work on a flat - incline and then decline, as this will work both his upper and lower chest muscles.

7. Strength Work

The following strength training exercises can be worked after the fielders have performed their CV aerobic workout, or on completely different days, totally depending on how much time a fielder has to perform his fitness training. The fielder should remember never work muscles when they are tired or sore, as this will lead to injury and negative results.

8. Lateral Pull Downs

The fielder should remember to pull the bar to the front of the body, aim for 3-4 sets, reducing the weight each time, aiming for 12-15 reps. Try and perform this routine with minimal rest between sets, keeping a smooth rate of 3-1-3. Keep your back straight and abdominal muscles contracted to avoid any forward movement from his waist.

If a fielder can work using a Swiss Ball, this will force him to fix his abdominal muscles, rather than having his knees under the machine restraints.

9. Rear Deltoid Pull

The fielder should perform 2-3 sets of 12-15 reps with a suitable weight by using the lower pulley of a cable machine perform. The fielder should remember that there is nothing wrong with either using a lighter weight or fewer reps with his weaker arm. He should avoid twisting the body in a 3-0-2 rate. If the fielder feels that his body is twisting, then he should perform this particular exercise seated by stressing his arms and elbows under appropriate angle rotation.

10. Inclined bench

This is yet another relevant aerobic exercises consisted of one set of 12–15 reps with light weight. The fielder should concentrate on good technique, and warming the chest muscles up. The fielder should follow this technique with 2-3 sets × 10 -12 reps dumbbell presses. The fielder should aim for a 3-0-2 workout rate, 3 sec's to lower the weight, then 2 sec's to lift. The fielder may work with a flat bench or a barbell if there is no availability of incline bench.

11. Standing Biceps

This exercises strengthens the arm muscles. This exercise may be performed by using either cable pulley or free weights. The fielder should keep the elbows tucked into the side, avoiding any swinging movement. The performer wish to work with his back against a wall, to totally isolate the biceps muscle, however, the fielder should always focus on keeping his elbows tucked into his sides.

By working with dumbbells, a fielder can perform a hammer action curl, however this is a harder movement, so the weight should be reduced. The fielder should aim to work for 2-3 sets of 10-12 reps in a 2-0-2 action.

12. Reverse Fly's

It is an superb exercise recommended for the fielders in order to developing their back muscles. The fielder should rest his body on either of his thigh or a bench to provide support to his lower back. The fielder should aim to perform three sets with a light weight for a high number of reps. The fielder should avoid any jerking action during the course of movement. The fielder should sit with his right hand shoulder facing towards a low pulley. He should hold a single stirrup connection in his right hand, having his arm bent to 90°, with his forearm parallel to the floor with the cable extend across his body.

The fielder should make himself sure that he should sit far enough away from the pulley, to prevent the cable in a smooth motion across his body so that his hand should finish by his opposite side. A fielder/perform should aim to work for 2 sets of 10-12 reps at a rate of 2-1-2.

13. Oblique and Abdominal Exercises

The fielders should use the abdominal workouts within the members area with a aim to start with the beginner session's and progress to working up to the advanced sessions by using both the Swiss Ball and Medicine Ball. Every fielder should work on this particular area in order to improve his speed, injury reduction and strength.

14. Lower Body Workout

The fielder should look at performing the lower body session, or lower body circuit ideally once a week. The fielder should not perform these sessions on the same day as either the upper body workout or his plyometric session. A fielder can perform these sessions on the same day as your CV aerobic workouts, and his abdominal sessions.

15. GYM EXERCISES

The fielder should create a healthier stronger body,

and should gain the knowledge on how to perform over 200 muscle and fitness exercises.

In order to test yourself, a fielder should monitor his progression. The best way to test one's progression is to establish an current fitness level then after the gap of every 8-12 weeks, the fielder should re-test yourself . With positive results in his test, the fielder can see improvements in his body's fitness.

If there is any negative results, the fielder. should obviously need to spend more time on that particular area by work out. There must be adequate accuracy and cleanliness in the tests performed, the fielder should maintain the previous test scores and records.

16. MINUTE WORKOUT

If there is unavailability of time or shortage of time, the fielder should perform a minute workout for short of time. During the short time period, the fielder used to pump those arms up for a quick photo shoot, this workout will help the fielder in keeping his arms, leg muscle up-to-date and will provide extra energy required for performing common fielding drills such as throwing, running, etc.

The fielder should not perform this exercise not more than 3 times a week. The fielder should perform this abdominal workout to help to develop the muscles.

There are individual fitness programmes mostly suitable for beginner, intermediate and advance level.

17. Biceps Weight Training Programme for Beginners

This sort of programme is recommended for beginners who are new to using weights. If a fielder need a harder workout, then he should perform biceps weight training programme according to his physique and· capability under the guidance of personal trainer and physicians.

18. Circuit Training

Usually, circuit training is one of the best ways to achieve physical fitness level. The fielders should perform this particular training under the guidance of a team physicians, coach in order to get the relevant results.

By performing cricket training programme, the fielder may improve his game by training with weights and plyometrics during the winter season and to get strength, speed and momentum in the course of his game during the summer season.

20. Walking

Walking is considered as the one of the best and simplest form of exercises that is recommended by almost every clinician, practitioners, physiotherapists etc., in order to gain speed, momentum and flexibilities among the various bodily joints particularly arms and leg muscles.

21. Warm-up

Every exercise and physical fitness programme begins with the warm-up and ends with the cool down. The fielders should perform warm-up in order to prepare himself for physically and mentally exercises. Warm-up reduces the chances of sports injuries as it already provides energy to the body and make the performer's body prepare to undergo strenuous exercises.

8

THE WICKETKEEPING

The wicketkeeper is the only specialist fielder in a team side. He has to perform tedious function of keeping behind the wickets and just keep watching the ball, collect it and get back to the bowler. He is the busiest player in the fielding team.

Generally, a wicketkeeper has to dress up with protective coverings such as hand gloves, leg pads, safety helmets, tooth protector, shin guards etc. The wicketkeeper is the one of the important members of the fielding team who used to encouraging his bowlers and fellow fielders all the time during the match.

The wicketkeeper has to perform various functions on the field in favour of his fielding team. The following are some of his functions:

1. The wicketkeeper has to move all the time he keeping the wickets.

2. He always encourages his bowler and fellow fielders and thus provide moral and psychological support to them.

3. The wicketkeeper has to keep stance by keeping his knees bent, crouch down, positioned slightly outside off stump, so that he has a clear view past the stumps.

4. While keeping the stance, the wicketkeeper should transfer his bodily weight on the front feet with keeping the head still and hands close together down the feet with the fingers pointing downwards.

5. One of the major functions of a wicketkeeper is to catch the ball either edge from the batsman's bat, glove, pad or from other sources. In order to take ordinary and extraordinary catches, the wicketkeeper has to undergo some catching techniques; he should adopt the correct stance at first, the wicketkeeper should rise after judging the bounce of the ball then he should move his feet and body to get into line with the ball. He should take the ball with fingers pointing downwards if the ball is below the chest height and in case the ball is higher then he should twist the head and body and take the ball with horizontal hands.

6. One of the important functions a wicketkeeper has to perform is the stumping. If a batsman misses the ball while attempting to play some loose stroke and steps outside his batting crease, the wicketkeeper has the chance to breaks the wickets/bails with the ball and the batsman is declared stumped out.

7. The team's special fielder i.e., wicketkeeper sometimes used to play key role in team's victory by performing some extraordinary catches, stumping behind the wickets.

8. A wicketkeeper is a keen player in any team. He should be a all-rounder specially should be able to play a long innings when the senior batsmen are out and his team is in critical condition.

The above mentioned are some of the important tasks that a wicketkeeper has to perform while behind the wickets or batting. Thus, a wicketkeeper is a key player in any team, he is a team's specialist and busiest fielder who has to move all the time behind the wickets. Beside a specialist fielder, a wicketkeeper is a useful batsman who sometimes play an important role in team's extraordinary victory.

In today's modern cricket in which the fast bowling gained its importance at peak the vision of a keeper is one, standing back lunging and diving to collect the speedy balls from the fast bowlers. Generally, one of the important aspects of wicketkeeping is to stand close to the stumps to the spinners and stand in line with the ball in case of the fast bowlers.

One of the ingredients of a efficient wicketkeeping is the appropriate stance that will play an important role in wicketkeeping. The wicketkeeper's stance should be well balanced. The wicketkeeper should evenly distributed his bodily weight on both feet. The gloves of the wicketkeeper should be in resting sequence i.e., downwards towards the ground. The wicketkeeper should concentrate on his standing position; he should not stand either too close or too far from the wickets because a wicketkeeper usually influences the position of the slip fielders. The wicketkeeper should stand at a distance at a point just the ball begins to drop towards the batsman.

The wicketkeeper should take his position around the off stump in order to have a clear vision of the ball coming from the bowler's end. The wicketkeeper should endeavour to pick the line of the delivery as early as possible. In wicketkeeping, anticipation played an important role to get success in wicketkeeping as it is called the key of wicketkeeping.

Whenever a wicketkeeper used to stand up to the stumps, he should make a insight into his mind i.e., he should imagine a image resembling to that of a semi circle at his working space behind the wickets. A good keeper used to stay close to the wickets in order to get ready to have a stumping chance whenever the batsman is used to play some loose strokes by step out of his crease and miss the ball.

A wicket keeper is always in the firing line and is never injury free for long. Some wicketkeepers used to keep the wickets with fractures in their fingers. To reduce the risk of injury, the wicketkeeper should never point their fingers at the ball. In order to reduce the risk of jarring, the wicketkeeper should endeavour himself to receive the ball and should not snatch the ball hastily.

One important thing that a wicketkeeper should concentrate on is, he should not rise from his stance too early. He should assume every delivery is coming at him even on the fastest of pitches its not easy but that is the test of a keeper, to concentrate hard for long periods of time.

A good wicketkeeper may dominant the game with his efficient wicketkeeping skills that can have a great effect on the team. It has also become the job of a keeper that he encourages the bowler and advises the captain from time to time for you are in the best position to study the game.

The wicketkeeper should be very alert for a possibility of a run out at all times. It is his responsibility to come up to the stumps whenever necessary.

In order to keep safe, a wicketkeeper should always stand well back at first on a pitch that he is not used to.

The wicketkeeper should make himself sure that he is standing in a position so that he can see the bowler run in and so that he is able to watch the ball all the way from the time that it leaves the bowler's hand. Whenever the wicketkeeper can, he should first make sure that the ball is "dead".

For the ball to be "dead", it must be taken and held in the wicketkeeper's gloves securely. If the ball hits the batter's pads and rolls away a few yards, the wicketkeeper should not stand still appealing for a possible LBW, he should run to get the ball.

The same applies if the ball hits the wickets when an attempt has been made to run out a batter who has made his ground. The wicketkeeper or another fielder near the wickets should not stand around appealing for a possible run-out if the ball is close-by.

The wicketkeeper should get the ball at first. If the ball has gone some distance away and another fielder has gone to collect it, then a wicketkeeper may have time to repair the wicket before the ball is thrown back.

The wicketkeeper used to replace the bails after they have been knocked off by the ball for instance after a throw-in in an attempt to run out a batter, or by the wicketkeeper, this particular situation is often called as *Repairing the Bails.* When the bails have been knocked off, as above, and the batters set off for another run on the overthrow, then the wicketkeeper should repair the wicket.

In fact, a wicketkeeper should only need to replace one bail to repair the wicket when the ball is still in play, and to knock that bail off when the ball is returned. When running to field a ball that has gone past the wicketkeeper in some way or other, he should throw off a glove so that he has a hand free to pick up the ball and to throw it in.

In order to help a fielder who is running to field a ball that has been hit into the outfield, the wicketkeeper should raise one arm so that the fielder can pick out the target easily when making the return throw.

In order to take the bails off for a stumping or a run-out, the wicketkeeper should always remember to use any part of the arm below the shoulder in order to remove the bail provided that he has the bail into that particular arm.

The wicketkeeper should encourage his team to cross over quickly by getting yourself quickly to the other end after the interval of each over.

9

WICKETKEEPING ESSENTIALS

The importance of wicket-keeping is emphasised by the fact that whilst there are 11 players to bat and several to bowl in a team, there is only one to keep wickets. On him falls the entire responsibility of accepting fine snicks and effecting stumpings and run-cuts as well as keeping byes down to a minimum.

While he is on the field, it is a whole time job, one for a true specialist. It is only possible for a player to become a good wicket keeper if he practise hard and applied correct techniques.

The following are some necessary ingredients that a wicketkeeper should possess of :

1. The wicketkeeper should have sharp eyesight, footwork and plenty of energy.

2. A wicket keeper has got to be properly equipped to give him maximum of comfort and freedom of movement, as well as minimum risk of injury.

3. The wicketkeeper should wear easy light and easy fitting boots properly spiked are essential as heavy boots will hamper quick movement.

4. The wicketkeeper should wear well fitting trousers that will reduce to a minimum the discomfort of

continuous bending.

5. A strong and well fitting abdominal protector must always be worn.

6. The pads should be light with a reasonable amount of padding and well protected in the region of the knee.

7. The top strap should be fairly loose to permit freedom of action when bending or moving quickly.

8. The wicketkeeper should wear soft chamois leather inner gloves in order to get extra protection and appropriate grip while handling the ball.

9. Gloves are as important to a wicket-keeper as a balanced bat to a batsman. A loose fitting pair with broad palms and roomy fingers is preferable. In modern gloves the fingers and thumbs are well protected with leather shields, and in addition, sponge rubber tips are inserted in each finger and thumb of the gloves.

10. Special attention should be given to the treatment of the rubber facing of the hands of the gloves to ensure that they are not smooth, but retentive. A good wicket-keeper should not allow his gloves to be worn by others lest the formation of the palm-fitting may be disturbed.

Position

Squatting position is recommended, with the seat very close to the ground and the weight evenly distributed as well as balanced between both feet. The back of the hands will initially be resting on the ground between the legs.

The advantage of this position is that it minimizes muscular strain and provides the best possible sight of the ball. The left foot is behind the middle and off stumps and the right will be parallel with it some distance away. Both feet will directly be pointing down the pitch. The body and head must be kept still, and it is of vital important that they stay down as long as possible, only rising to meet the rise of the ball off the pitch.

Stance

The wicket-keeper's stance should be such that he is comfortable and there is no strain, that he can get the best possible view of bowler right from the time he takes a start and delivers the ball, that the ball is collected with the minimum of movement, that he is so close to the wicket that after taking the ball, he can comfortably break the wicket.

Placement

A wicket-keeper must stand either right up or right back. He has to stand back to any bowling above medium-pace or to medium-paced bowling on very fast or sticky wickets. By standing in this position, it is easy for him to take catches either on the off or leg side off faster kicking deliveries. In general, he will aim at so positioning himself that the good length ball will reach him just after it starts to drop in its trajectory after pitching.

Taking Balls on the Leg-Side

Stumping from a delivery outside or over the leg-stump is the most difficult part of wicket-keeping, because the batsman's body obscures the view of the ball for a fraction of a second, as the keeper moves across to take it. Moving speedily across to the correct position on the leg-side and accurate judgment of the course of ball off the wicket are the hallmarks of a first class wicket keeper. Whatever the type of bowler, a wicket-keeper must always adopt his normal stance.

When a ball appears to be pitched outside the leg-stump, his first move is to step across just outside its line of flight, thus enabling him to take the ball on the inside of the body; this tends to make a move for stumping easier and quicker, and also gives an extra allowance, if the ball is touched, for the keeper to take the catch. As soon as the outer foot reaches its new position the weight of the body should be transferred to it, and the other foot should then be brought across to make certain of correct balance. Once the ball is safely taken a stumping may be made smartly removing the bails with outstretched hands.

Taking Balls on Off-Side

If a ball is pitched on or just outside the off-stump, it is not necessary to move more than slightly from the original stance. As the ball leaves the pitch the weight of the body is transferred to the right foot and the keeper rises from the crouching position. The fingers point to the ground and on taking the ball the body turns slightly to allow the gloves to be brought back to give with the ball.

This yielding of the hands with the ball will ensure well settling of the ball into the hands. Do not try to grab at the ball. Stumping from a ball just outside or over the off stump is effected by bringing the body well behind the line of flight of the ball. Then with a quick arm movement the bails are removed. If the ball is well wide of the off-stump the right foot must move parallel to the crease and as near to the line of flight as possible, and the left foot is taken near the right foot to keep the balance.

Run-Outs

One of the most important jobs of a wicket-keeper is

the taking of returns from the field, especially where a run-out is possible. Returns, many of them not accurate come at all heights and at all speeds and the man with the gloves must be very active and accurate in his catching.

Returns from the field should be over the stumps and on the full, especially when a run out is attempted. Otherwise, the wicket-keeper will probably find that he has to move backwards to take the ball on the bounce off the grass, or reach upwards to take the ball if it is thrown too high, or leave the stumps to take an inaccurate return. All of these movements waste vital time in taking off the bails, and none of them would be necessary if the throwing was accurate.

There are occasions when a return on the bounce is justified where the distance is great or where the fieldsman is not a strong thrower. In each of these cases, the returns on the full would be lofted, and this would involve a little, and possibly vital, waste of time. But in all cases where the return is not on the full, the bounce should take the ball into the wicket-keeper's hands directly over the stumps. Finally, a wicket-keeper must keep really fit. And unless he does so, he cannot hope to command through a long day in the field the vigilant concentration and sustained activity which his job demands and which will mean so much to his side.

Keeping Wickets to Slow and Medium-Pace Bowlers

Keeping wickets to all types of bowling demands intense concentration and constant alertness, but keeping to slow spin bowling is not only the most difficult, but at the same time the most interesting. Good slow bowlers can do so much with the ball, that wicket-keepers must learn to detect which spin the bowler has imparted whilst the ball is in the air.

To wait until the ball has pitched is risky, as spin increases its speed after it hits the pitch and if the wicket-keeper has not judged the break correctly he will not be in the correct position, and consequently will have to move very hurriedly to get behind the ball or reach for it. In either case it is likely to beat him altogether, or he may fumble at it.

Slow bowlers, as a rule, operate into a breeze which helps the wicket keeper to pick which way the ball will turn, whilst it is actually on its way. Leg spin into a wind tends to cause the ball to float towards the leg, and conversely the off-spinner or the googly tends to swerve away to the off. But flight variations are not so noticeable on calm days and as good slow bowlers can bowl leg breaks, googlies and top-spinners with almost the same action, it is necessary for a wicket-keeper to learn to detect the difference before the ball pitches.

The wicketkeeper usually have wider opportunity to look at the bowler's variation because from his position he is in a better condition to judge the bowler's deliveries and hence able to take necessary actions. He may become quite capable of detecting slight differences in grip or wrist action, and with practice he may be able to see the spin of the ball in the air; in some cases, he may have to rely on some sign from the bowler, but obviously any sign is useless unless it is not detected by the batsman. Whatever his method, he must get to the stage, where he can detect all the variations of all his bowlers, if he is to be a top class wicket-keeper.

Wicket-Keeping to Fast and Medium Bowlers

It is the tendency for a wicket-keeper to stand back to fast bowlers and it is rare for him to stand up to the stumps even for the fast medium bowlers. It is more practical that he should do this. If he stands up to the wicket he is likely to misjudge the course of the ball off the pitch, especially if the bowler is getting lift off a lively wicket, or if a new ball is swinging a good deal, or if a delivery is on or outside the leg stump; and this is likely to lead to missing or fumbling the ball with resulting byes, or missing of vital snicks, or even injury to the wicket-keepers from a hit on the fingers, arms or body by a ball which he has slightly misjudged. Rarely do batsmen move out of the crease to play the fastest bowlers, as they have no time to do so, and it follows that opportunities for stumpings are rare off these bowlers.

Therefore, a wicket-keeper generally stands back at a distance where the ball will come off the wicket to him about waist high, and in this position he has ample time to sight the ball, move to it and take it cleanly, even though it swings or be snicked either on the leg or off-side. Each time a ball is played to a fieldsman the wicket-keeper has got to move up to the stumps to take the return and be in position for any possible run out.

10

RULES OF FIELDING

THE FIELD

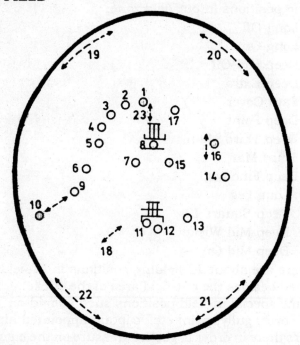

Generally, the cricket field is divided into three sections:
1. Out-Field;
2. In-Field;
3. Close-In-Field.

The captain usually arrange his team members into the fielding positions by discussing with the striking bowler. The fielding captain according to the match strategies and circumstances and advice from the bowler used to spread his fielders into relevant positions depending upon the calibre and capacities of the fielders.

There are 13 fielding positions in outfield zone situated at the outermost area of the cricket ground. Usually in one day cricket, in order to save the boundaries and holding the catches, the captain used to arrange his fielders during the last ten overs when the batsmen are playing with their best form. The following are the 13 fielding positions in out-field zone:

1. Long-Off
2. Long-On
3. Deep Mid-Off
4. Deep Extra
5. Exta Cover
6. Deep Point
7. Deep Third Main
8. Third Man
9. Deep Fine Leg
10. Long Leg
11. Deep Square Leg
12. Deep Mid Wicket
13. Deep Mid On

There are about 12 fielding positions in In-field zone situated besides the out-field area of the cricket ground. At some special in-field positions such as mid-on, short extra cover, gully, point etc., captain appointed his best fielders there in order to get the pressure on the batsmen.

The following are the 12 fielding positions in in-field zone:

1. Mid-off
2. Mid-on
3. Mid Wicket

4. Short Extra Cover
5. Cover Point
6. Backward Point
7. Point
8. Gully
9. Short Third Man
10. Short Fine Leg
11. Backward Square Leg
12. Square Leg

There are about 12 fielding positions in Close-In-Field zone situated besides and close to the cricket pitch. Usually, team's best and specialist fielders get positioned in some of the important close-in-field positions such as slips, silly point, short mid-on, forward short leg etc. During the first fifteen overs in one day cricket, the fielding captain used to appoint his team' specialist fielders in some close-in-field positions with the motive to get the batsmen out and cease them from scoring runs in the form of singles.

The following are the 12 fielding positions in close-in-field zone:

1. First Slip
2. Second Slip
3. Third Slip
4. Fourth Slip
5. Silly Point
6. Silly Mid-off
7. Short Mid-off
8. Short Mid-on
9. Silly Mid-on
10. Forward Short Leg
11. Backward Short Leg
12. Leg Slip

EQUIPMENTS
Protective Equipment
Except the wicketkeeper, no team members on the

field are permitted to wear gloves or external leg guards. Only brief protection for the hand or fingers may be worn only with the permission of the umpires.

Shoes

The fielders should always wear light weigh footwear as they used to run and move all the times on the field during the play. The appropriate care must be taken to wear light footwear with protection at the toe and with the right sole for the surface you are playing.

(1) On turf wickets and where the wicket is wet and slippery, shoes with rubber soles and metal spikes in front are recommended for a secure grip while running, turning and playing shots.

(2) On matting and other artificial surfaces, shoes with rubber spiked soles will be the most comfortable.

The following things should be keep in mind while selecting the shoe:

(i) The foot should not move inside the shoe while landing. It is recommended that a bowler wear two pairs of thick socks made of cotton, jute or wool depending on the weather conditions.

(ii) The shoe must be spiked and comfortably fitting with ten to twelve metal spikes. It must be light with well padded inner soles. The ankle should be cut higher helping to support the ankle during the delivery stride.

Thigh Guards

Like the batsman, the team's specialist fielder, wicketkeeper too used to wear thigh guards in order to protect his thighs from the pace bowling from the fast bowlers and pacers.

Pad

Usual term for the device known as a leg-guard only in cricket catalogues, a cane and canvas structure strapped to the lower leg to protect it against the impact of the ball. Also worn by the batsman.

Abdominal Protector

A vital piece of cricketing protective equipment, also known as 'box'. It is worn by the wicketkeeper, close-in-field fielder fielding at the suicidal fielding positions like silly point etc.

Hat

In order to protect from the sunlight and making the ease while holding high catch, the fielders used to wear hat according to their preferences. The batsmen too used to wear hat while facing spinners and slow bowlers.

FIELDERS

Good fielding is very important. A good fielding side can save twenty runs or more in an innings of twenty overs. So, make sure that you learn all the correct methods of fielding a ball, like the long barrier position. And if you cannot yet throw a ball very far, then try to throw it, at least, in a straight line.

A fielder should be well versed in fielding skills, and drills and all the main fielding positions that there are, so that when he is asked to go and field in that position he will know where it is.

A ball is in play when the bowler has taken the first stride of his run-up. From thereon, all fielders should keep absolutely quiet until the ball has been delivered and the batter has either played a stroke or let the ball go by. If a batter happens to hit his wicket before the ball has arrived to him, the fielders should not make any sort of appeal until the ball has been played or has gone past the wickets.

When the fielders are fielding, they should concentrate all the time on their fielding. In order to avoid collision among the fellow fielders and confusion pertaining fielding, all the fielders should call and address each other while getting, holding and throwing the ball from the batsmen.

If a fielder is in a position to observe the ball, he should watch where the ball pitches when it is bowled and watch the movement the batter makes with his bat and his feet. This will give the fielder some idea of the sort of stroke the batter will try to make and he can start to move in anticipation.

Whether catching or fielding a ball, watch it all the way until it is safely into your hands. Never hold on to a ball after fielding it. As soon as the fielders have got the ball securely into their hands, they should return it immediately to the wicket-keeper or the bowler. But when the fielder used to take a catch, they should hold on to the ball securely for a few seconds. The fielder should never throw it up in the air in triumph or toss it straight away to another player.

When going for a catch, if the fielder know that he did not take the ball cleanly, (meaning that it touched the ground first), then the fielder should indicate to the umpire and the batter that he did not catch the ball.

If one of his fellow fielders is in the process of taking a catch, the fielder should not shout out anything until he has safely held the ball. A very dangerous situation can arise when two or more fielders run to catch a ball that has been hit high into the air. Making the right decision so as to avoid players colliding and injuring themselves is not at all easy, but try to remember these general rules:

i. A fielder who is certain of taking the catch should call out, "Mine", as early as possible. Any other fielder also running towards the ball should then stop still.

ii. If he can do so, the captain should shout out the name of the fielder who is to take the catch, especially if two fielders call "Mine" more or less at the same time.

iii. The ball should be left to the fielder in whose direction the ball is travelling.

HIGH CATCH

There is hardly a more exciting sight at a cricket ground than when a ball is high in the sky and a fielder is getting under it. Brings the crowd alive. Can be quite unnerving for a fielder though for it is quite a while that he stays under the ball, ample time for all kinds of thoughts to run through the mind.

A fielder's true test are observed when he is taking a skier or high catch. A coach often puts a new student through this test. The position shown above is ideal in taking the catch. Watch how the fielder has brought one leg slightly in front to balance the body. Again do not stay on the heels. It also helps to react quickly if there is fumble. Eyes on the ball at all times irrespective of the bumps you might feel off the ground .

The fielder should perform high catch by the cup of the hand at around the chest height is ideal. If a fielder is taking a running skier very vital that he run on his toes.

Instead of sprinting hard a balanced, gliding run is preferable, only because it keeps your head steady which mean your eyes are steady and that means a steady vision of the ball.

Nearly all cricketers have difficulty in catching a ball that comes out of the sun. Practise catching a high ball by extending an arm in the air and spreading out your hand as if to blot out the sun. When the ball is a few feet away bring both hands together quickly for the catch.

FIELDING THE BALL

A fielder used to field the ball hit by the batsmen or from any other sources viz., leg byes, over throw byes etc.

Fielders need the ability to sustain a concentrated effort for a 6 hour plus period without fatigue, in sometimes very warm conditions. Their bodies must be capable of explosive bursts at any given time - such as racing for a ball, jumping for a catch. The fielders should aim to keep their body moving whilst on the pitch, walking and stretching the muscles whenever possible. The fielders should keep their mind busy by visualizing exactly what they will do when the ball comes towards them.

The following are the functions that a fielder has to perform while fielding on the ground :

1. Return the ball over the stumps
2. Anticipate the ball at all times
3. Anticipate the bounce of the ball i.e. wet/quick
4. Back up all returns to the wicket
5. Mark your spot in the field and walk in, unless in close.
6. Provide verbal and non verbal assistance to your team mates.
7. Walk in with the bowler when fielding in the out field.
8. Retain balance before throwing the ball.

FIELDING PRINCIPLES

The following are coaching tips and principles for the fielders :

1. The fielder should not stand in front of the square leg umpire. He might not be able to see anything if there is an appeal. Stand to one side either in front or behind him.
2. When fielding on the boundary stand with your feet just inside the line. Do not walk in with the bowler. Instead be on your toes ready to move diagonally either to your left or right.
3. Always help the umpire when you can. For example, if a ball touches or crosses the boundary line and the umpire has difficulty in seeing it, then signal to the umpire. Remember umpires are there to help players, too.
4. Even though the ball has not been hit your way, you must watch it all the time that it is in play. That means, until it has been returned securely into the hands of the wicketkeeper or the bowler. The ball then becomes "dead".
5. When returning the ball to the bowler, keep it in the air. This is very important if the ground is wet.

If the bowler is a long way away, throw the ball to another fielder close by you so that he can return it to the bowler.

6. The fielder should not stand too close with the fellow fielders in order to avoid collision with each other while running, collecting and holding the speedy ball.

7. When a ball has been struck deep into the outfield and clear of any fielders, then at least two fielders should chase after the ball.

8. The fielder should not throw the ball in the air out of the sun as there is a greater chance of the over throw and put some extra runs to the opponent's score board.

9. If you field a ball and it is obvious that the batters are not intending to take a run, do not throw the ball back to the bowler until the bowler is clear of the non-striking batter and the umpire. They might get hit!

10. The fielders should not make appeals for lbw if they are fielding in the positions where the clear vision of the ball is not visible and there is not clear cut vision of the pitch.

FIELD PLACEMENT

There is not thorough specification pertaining cricket field; it is not standardised. There are several named field positions, and the fielding captain uses different combinations of them for tactical reasons. There are also further descriptive words to specify variations on the positions labelled by simple names, so that any position in which a fielder stands can be described.

OUTFIELDERS

Boundary Fielders

Boundary fielders are usually the bowlers – less-agile movers dispatched to deeper pastures.

The Slide Stop

The slide stop has really been in vogue the last ten

years or so.

Throwing

Throwing has always been a weak link in English cricket – there seem to be few players who can whizz an exocet into the keeper's gloves from 60 yards.

CLOSE FIELDERS

Slips

Few overs are bowled in a Test match without at least one man in the slips. Slip is probably the most important fielding position in the game.

Gully

Gully means gap, this particular fielding position is named as gully because gully fieldsman has to field in the gap between slip and cover. The gully fielder will tend to vary where he stand according to the pitch and the batsman.

Short Leg and Silly Point

This is the most suicidal fielding position where the fielder is positioned at the batsman's backside. As this is the most risky area, the fielder has to wear some safety equipments in order to protect himself and avoid injuries. Generally, the fielder is equipped with safety helmet.

Cover Point

Usually, a team's sprightliest fielder is stationed at cover point. It's a vital position as most defensive shots go in this direction, and you can expect batsmen to look for quick singles in that area.

Fielding in the Ring

Any man fielding 'in the ring' – i.e. the positions about 25 yards from the bat, which are there to stop the batsmen taking easy singles – is expected to attack the ball.